COLLECTING
POKÉMON ®

Jeffrey B. Snyder

Schiffer
Publishing Ltd

To kids of all ages everywhere.

DISCLAIMER

This book is not published, authorized by or associated in any way with the owners of the trademarks, characters and other graphics depicted in this reference guide. According to the U.S. Patent and Trademark Office records: "NINTENDO", "POKEMON" and "GAME BOY" are U.S. registered trademarks of Nintendo of America Inc. and "GOTTA CATCH 'EM ALL" and "PIKACHU" are pending trademark U.S. applications of Nintendo of America Inc.; and "WIZARDS OF THE COAST" is a U.S. registered trademark of Wizards of the Coast, Inc. "GAME FREAK" is believed to be a trademark of Nintendo of America Inc. or a related company. It is believed that all of the other character names and designs are trademarks of Nintendo of America Inc. or a related company.

The copyrights to the characters and other graphics depicted in this collector's reference guide are copyrighted by Nintendo of America Inc. or by a related company. This book is for the use, information, and entertainment of collectors. None of the trademark registrants, nor copyright holders have authorized this book, nor furnished, nor approved of any of the information contained herein. This book in no way attempts to infringe on any intellectual property of any party and is not to be used for any purpose other than as a reference guide.

Copyright © 2000 by Schiffer Publishing
Library of Congress Catalog Card Number: 99-054506

All rights reserved. No part of this work may be reproduced or used in any form or by any means—graphic, electronic, or mechanical, including photocopying or information storage and retrieval systems—without written permission from the copyright holder.
    "Schiffer," "Schiffer Publishing Ltd. & Design," and the "Design of pen and ink well" are registered trademarks of Schiffer Publishing Ltd.

Cover design by Bruce Waters
Book design by Blair Loughrey
Type set in Zurich/SkidoosD/Beesknees
1 2 3 4

ISBN: 0-7643-1075-5
Printed in China

Published by Schiffer Publishing Ltd.
4880 Lower Valley Road
Atglen, PA 19310
Phone: (610) 593-1777; Fax: (610) 593-2002
E-mail: Schifferbk@aol.com
Please visit our web site catalog at
www.schifferbooks.com
or write for a free catalog.
This book may be purchased from the publishe
Please include $3.95 for shipping.

In Europe, Schiffer books are distributed by
Bushwood Books
6 Marksbury Ave.
Kew Gardens
Surrey TW9 4JF England
Phone: 44 (0)208 392-8585
Fax: 44 (0)208 392-9876
E-mail: Bushwd@aol.com
Free postage in the UK. Europe: air mail at cost

Please try your bookstore first.

We are interested in hearing from authors with book ideas on related subjects.

Contents

Acknowledgments

No book is ever completed alone. I want to personally thank all of the people who made this guide possible. They contributed their time, information, and collections to the project. Without them, this book would not exist. Special thanks to my expert contributors: Michael W. Snyder, Adam Whiteford, Matthew Whiteford, and Zapp! Comics, Cards, Toys, which may be reached through the www.zapptoys.com e mail address. Michael also patiently read through the text to make sure I had the details right.

Thanks also to Doug Congdon-Martin, who also read through the text. He provided the invaluable perspective of the confused adult who has absolutely no idea what this Pokémon® business is all about. Thanks to Peter Schiffer for clearing the way for this project and to the talented staff at the publishing house who gave this "pocket tome" its character. Finally, a special thank you to all the readers. You are the ones who keep these books alive!

Introduction

Exactly what are Pokémon® and where do they come from? American parents—and others who have yet to catch any Pokémon—have been asking that question in greater numbers every day since September 1998, when Nintendo first sent its popular Japanese "Pocket Monsters" to the United States. Pokémon—the fictional monsters who populate the games, videos, comics and television series of the same name—include over 150 competitive beasts with special powers, battling one another under the direction of human trainers. Many of these creatures are thick on the ground, while others are less common, and a fabled few are rarely seen. With proper training and battle experience, many Pokémon will evolve from one form into another, larger and more powerful form. The trainers seek to capture, master, and battle all of these creatures against the beasts other trainers have collected. The trainer who captures, masters, and successfully battles every monstrous Pokémon becomes a Pokémon Master.

"What the heck are Pokémon?" you might ask. Since September 1998, lots of people have been wondering. — *Pikachu Shocks Back* #1, Pokémon comic book by Viz Comics, 1999. $3-4 CRP — Read on and I'll explain.

Above: A 2-Player Starter Set (a.k.a. "Base Set") by Wizards of the Coast. *Courtesy of the Michael W. Snyder Collection.*

Right: Pokémon Game Boy Red cartridge by Nintendo. $30 CRP

In the real world, kids most often seek to capture all the creatures they can in the trading card game, the Game Boy hand held video game, and the N64 Pokémon Snap home video game. Game players and collectors alike have taken up the quest to capture every Pokémon monster from the trading card game, some of which are quite rare and elusive. Bagging a Charizard Trading Card with a holographic foil background is a real accomplishment!

Pokémon initially arrived in the United States as an animated cartoon television show that rapidly captured the attention of children. Encouraged by the excitement the show generated, Nintendo quickly dispensed Pokémon video games, trading cards, comic books, books, home videos and candy. Of these, the trading card game and the Game Boy video game have been the most popular. Pre-teens everywhere are eager to return to school in the fall to see which trading cards their schoolmates have, what they will trade, and who they can match wits against...after classes are over of course! (Lippman 1999)

The game quickly caught on with young gamesters and collectors for a number of reasons. It is ever changing, with new trading cards and characters added periodically to the line. It is also portable (in either card or Game Boy format, fitting neatly into a pocket), quick to play, affordable, and the trading cards or characters may be swapped back and forth. For parents, the game is a pleasant alternative to much of the standard fare offered today. There is no sex or gore, combatants may be defeated but will return to fight another day rather than die, and the monsters are, well, for the most part pretty cuddly characters.

Charizard Holographic Foil Trading Card, Evolution Stage 2, Base Set: LV. 76, #6, 4/102, Rare. *Courtesy of www.zapptoys.com* $35-40; $80-90 Edition 1

A Little History

In 1995, Ninetendo introduced Japanese children to its Pocket Monters role playing game for the Game Boy video game system. The response was enthusiastic. The game was quickly followed by toys, comic books, trading cards and an animated television series. Within two years, Nintendo had released 151 of the fiesty little beasts into the hands of kids all over the island nation. However, concerned that the animation style and format of the game would not go over well on foreign soil, Nintendo was unwilling to venture into the American market until 1998.

Above: Japanese movable Pocket Monster toy. *Courtesy of www.zapptoys.com*

Right: Japanese Paras Trading Card from the Jungle Set, Common. *Courtesy of the Adam Whiteford Collection.*

Above: Japanese Pikachu pencil topper by Tomy. Japanese Pokémon products may be purchased through specialty dealers. These folks may be found advertised in any number of specialty toy magazines available at newstands and bookstores around the nation.

Left: Nintendo was unsure American kids would enjoy Japanese comic art and animation styles. This page is from the comic book *Pikachu Shocks Back* #1 (volume one of a four volume series).

In September 1998, the company was convinced to take its first tentative steps into the American market. Reversing the Japanese release strategy, Nintendo began with the Pokémon (the name Pocket Monster was already in use by an American firm so the name was shortened to Pokémon) animated television series. This was followed quickly by the Pokémon video game, trading cards and all the rest. In November 1999, Pokémon took to the big screen in America as well with "Pokémon the Movie: Mewtwo Strikes Back." In Japan, in 1998, this film outsold the American import "Godzilla" by a large margin.

There are many thousands of items decorated with Pokémon characters to date. I will only be dealing with the most collectible of those toys, games, and comic books. The scads of give-aways, stickers, and school supplies have not been included. That would make a volume too large for mere humans to handle. Left: 36 Pokémon Trading Cards on the back of an Oscar Mayer Lunchables box. Once cut out, these cards have hints on how to deal with pesky Pokémon on the back. Top center: a Pokémon eraser. Right: Pokémon Temporary Tatoo Body Stickers ($2 CRP [Current Retail Price]). The loose cards and eraser are courtesy of the Matthew Whiteford collection.

Pokémon keychain with one of several possible Pokémon monsters to capture and release. This example holds Charmeleon. The other available monsters are shown on the back of the box. This keychain was produced by Basic Fun. *Courtesy of www.zapptoys.com* $5-6 CRP

Today, many thousands of Pokémon related products flood the American market. Hasbro is the master toy licensee, Wizards of the Coast carries the license to provide the trading card game, Topps entered the market with a line of Pokémon cards in August 1999, Grand Toys International produces Pokémon balls, school supplies and kites in abundance, and Toymax International produces Pokémon candy! Needless to say, there is something out there for every collector and enthusiast. In fact, catching all the Pokémon products in America today might be too great a challenge for even the most accomplished Pokémon Master. (Lippman 1999)

Here are the 150 Pokémon monsters, ordered by their "monster numbers." If you wanna catch 'em all, you gotta know 'em all!

#01 Bulbasaur	#53 Persian	#105 Marowak
#02 Ivysaur	#54 Psyduck	#106 Hitmonlee
#03 Venusaur	#55 Golduck	#107 Hitmonchan
#04 Charmander	#56 Mankey	#108 Lickitung
#05 Charmeleon	#57 Primeape	#109 Koffing
#06 Charizard	#58 Growlithe	#110 Weezing
#07 Squirtle	#59 Arcanine	#111 Rhyhorn
#08 Wartortle	#60 Poliwag	#112 Rhydon
#09 Blastoise	#61 Poliwhirl	#113 Chansey
#10 Caterpie	#62 Poliwrath	#114 Tangela
#11 Metapod	#63 Abra	#115 Kangaskhan
#12 Butterfree	#64 Kadabra	#116 Horsea
#13 Weedle	#65 Alakazam	#117 Seadra
#14 Kakuna	#66 Machop	#118 Goldeen
#15 Beedrill	#67 Machoke	#119 Seaking
#16 Pidgey	#68 Machamp	#120 Staryu
#17 Pidgeotto	#69 Bellsprout	#121 Starmie
#18 Pidgeot	#70 Weepinbell	#122 Mr. Mime
#19 Rattata	#71 Victreebel	#123 Scyther
#20 Raticate	#72 Tentacool	#124 Jynx
#21 Spearow	#73 Tentacruel	#125 Electabuzz
#22 Fearow	#74 Geodude	#126 Magmar
#23 Ekans	#75 Graveler	#127 Pinsir
#24 Arbok	#76 Golem	#128 Tauros
#25 Pikachu	#77 Ponyta	#129 Magikarp
#26 Raichu	#78 Rapidash	#130 Gyarados
#27 Sandshrew	#79 Slowpoke	#131 Lapras
#28 Sandslash	#80 Slowbro	#132 Ditto
#29 Nidoran♀	#81 Magnemite	#133 Eevee
#30 Nidorina	#82 Magneton	#134 Vaporeon
#31 Nidoqueen	#83 Farfetch'd	#135 Jolteon
#32 Nidoran♂	#84 Doduo	#136 Flareon
#33 Nidorino	#85 Dodrio	#137 Porygon
#34 Nidoking	#86 Seel	#138 Omanyte
#35 Clefairy	#87 Dewgong	#139 Omastar
#36 Clefable	#88 Grimer	#140 Kabuto
#37 Vulpix	#89 Muk	#141 Kabutops
#38 Ninetales	#90 Shellder	#142 Aerodactyl
#39 Jigglypuff	#91 Cloyster	#143 Snorlax
#40 Wigglytuff	#92 Gastly	#144 Articuno
#41 Zubat	#93 Haunter	#145 Zapdos
#42 Golbat	#94 Gengar	#146 Moltres
#43 Oddish	#95 Onix	#147 Dratini
#44 Gloom	#96 Drowzee	#148 Dragonair
#45 Vileplume	#97 Hypno	#149 Dragonite
#46 Paras	#98 Krabby	#150 Mewtwo
#47 Parasect	#99 Kingler	
#48 Venonat	#100 Voltorb	
#49 Venomoth	#101 Electrode	Please note that another
#50 Diglett	#102 Exeggcute	rare Pokémon has made
#51 Dugtrio	#103 Exeggutor	several appearances in the
#52 Meowth	#104 Cubone	U.S. to date — #151 Mew.

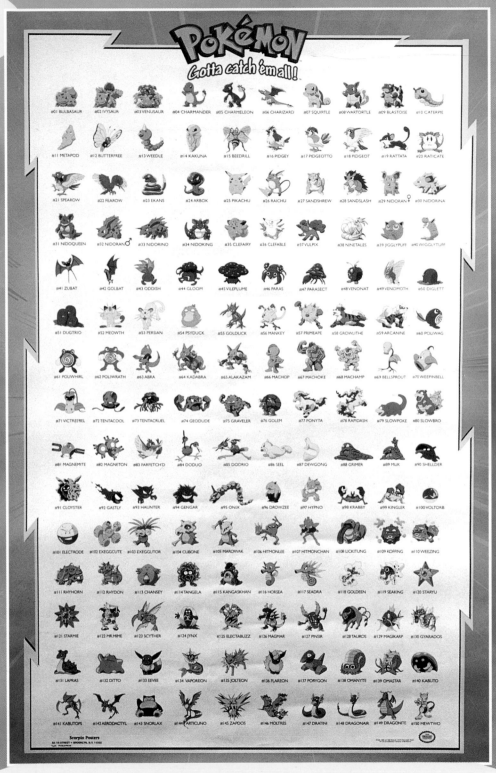

Here they are. All of the first 150 Pokémon, for everybody that has to know! Not shown is the elusive #151 Mew Pokémon, who may be glimpsed in Nintendo's Pokémon Snap game for the Nintendo 64 home video game system. This poster, measuring 34.5" x 22" and was produced by Scorpio Posters. *Courtesy of the Matthew Whiteford Collection.* $3-4 CRP

About the Prises

The pricing found here is in United States dollars. Prices are known to vary immensely, not only based on whether an item is in mint condition or in its original packaging, but also on the location of the market and the enthusiasms of the collecting community at any particular moment. Prices in the Midwest differ from those in the West or East, and those at specialty shops, in dealer's catalogs, and toy or hobby shops vary from those at conventions.

All of these factors make it impossible to create absolutely accurate price listings, but a guide to realistic pricing may be offered. These values are not provided to set prices in the collectibles marketplace, but rather to generally satisfy that intense curiosity we all have about what anything and everything is worth as well as to specifically give readers an idea of how much any particular item displayed here might set them back, should they decide to seek it out.

Pokémon Collectibles to Cotch

Here is a sampling of the most collectible Pokémon products available today. This book concentrates on the trading card game as that is the driving force behind the American Pokémon experience.

Pokémon Trading Cord Game

In the 1990s, trading card games have become very popular in the U.S. The trail for the Pokémon Trading Card Game was blazed by Magic: The Gathering (c. 1993), Star Trek: The Next Generation Customizable Card Game (1994), and the Star Wars Customizable Card Game (1995), among others . As with its predecessors, the Pokémon Trading Card Game has a variety of card decks and booster packs. The basic Pokémon Trading Card Game deck has sixty cards. Booster packs of eleven cards each are available to supplement the basic deck with rarer and more desirable cards. Expansion decks and theme decks further increase the diversity of the the basic deck, allowing players to design custom playing decks that best suit their personalities. (Snyder 1999, 126; Snyder 1999a, 148; Brokaw et al. 1999, 7)

Components of a Pokémon trading card game. A Base Set, Theme Deck, cards, coin, and damage counters. *Courtesy of the Michael W. Snyder, Adam Whiteford, and Matthew Whiteford Collections.*

The Pokémon Trading Card Game also differentiates between first edition cards and from later printings. This, combined with the rarity of some cards and the holographic foil backgrounds used on a select few, helps ensure that these game cards will not only provide an entertaining pastime but will also become worthy collectibles.

As with the best games, the basic rules and goals are straight forward but the strategies for winning may be quite complex. Assisting the players are rules printed on the card faces for the various Pokémon characters. Components needed for game play include one sixty card deck, a coin, and colored damage counters. All these are provided with the basic decks. (Gutschera 1998, 4)

Game coin from the Pokémon Base Set. Heads (Vileplume) and tails. *Courtesy of the Michael W. Snyder Collection.* NP

THE GAME

Here is a short explanation of the game for those who have never played, without going into all of the rule details. The Pokémon card game is a two-player game. Each player faces the other across a table. Each player has a 60 card deck.

To begin the game, players shuffle their decks, set aside six cards as prizes, and remove seven cards with which to play. From these, each player selects one Pokémon monster to do battle. The player may have up to five benched Pokémon in reserve to replace the battling Pokémon as the need arises. Several of the cards chosen will likely be Energy or Trainer cards that support the battling Pokémon.

Machop Trading Card, Basic Pokémon, Base Set: LV. 20, #66, 52/102, Common. *Courtesy of the Michael W. Snyder Collection.* $1-2

Above: Fighting Energy Trading Card, Base Set: 97/102. *Courtesy of the Michael W. Snyder Collection.* $0.50-0.55

Right: Super Energy Removal Trainer Trading Card: 79/102, Rare. *Courtesy of the Michael W. Snyder Collection.* $5-6

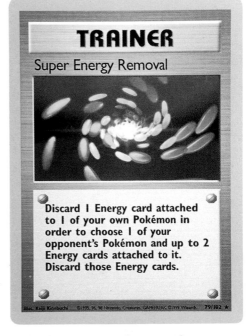

The player's cards are arranged in a particular way. Each player first puts aside the previously mentioned six Pokémon cards as prizes. These prizes are placed face down to the player's left. To the player's right are both the remainder of the deck and the discard pile for Pokémon monsters that have been knocked out during battle and for energy or trainer cards taken out of play. Immediately in front of each player is "the bench." The bench contains Pokémon monsters awaiting their turn at battle. In the middle is the active Pokémon, the monster doing battle with the opponent's active Pokémon.

The game is turn based. Each player takes a turn, strengthening his or her hand by drawing cards from the deck and battling with the opponent. The attacks each Pokémon may perform, the damage inflicted upon the opponent's Pokémon as a result of an attack, and any penalties for the attack are printed on each Pokémon card. Each player hopes, through a series of attacks, to knock out all of his opponent's Pokémon monsters, one after another. The game moves back and forth between the two opponents until one player wins.

A player wins the game in one of three ways: by taking his or her sixth prize card (one prize card is taken every time one of the opponent's Pokémon is knocked out), by defeating the opponent's last "in-play" Pokémon (a player is allowed six in-play Pokémon to compete with at any given moment), or by "decking" the opponent (no cards remain in his or her deck to pull from to continue play).

Are you more confused now than when you started? Oh well, those *are* the basics of the game. There are many rules and strategies guiding game play, as any dedicated Pokémon gamester will surely tell you.

Here is how the Pokémon trading cards should be set up for a game. Your opponent will have his or her cards arranged in the same way across the table from you. Left to right: six prize cards (top left), active Pokémon (center), five benched Pokémon (bottom, the most you can have in your bench), your deck (top right) and your discards (bottom right). *Courtesy of the Michael W. Snyder Collection.*

THE DECKS, EXPANSION SETS, AND BOOSTER PACKS

Several different deck types are currently offered for this game. Included among them are the Pokémon Two-Player Starter Set (or Base Set) and the Pokémon Brushfire, Overgrowth, Zap, Water Blast and Blackout pre-constructed theme decks. The starter set introduces beginners to the game and the theme decks move experienced players into more complex play.

Above: A 2-Player Starter Set by Wizards of the Coast. *Courtesy of the Michael W. Snyder Collection.*

Right: Brushfire Theme Deck. *Courtesy of www.zapptoys.com* $15-16 MIP

Right: Overgrowth Theme Deck by Wizards of the Coast. *Courtesy of the Michael W. Snyder Collection.* $15-16 MIP

Below: Water Blast Theme Deck for the Jungle Expansion Set. *Courtesy of www.zapptoys.com* $20-22 MIP

Blackout Theme Deck. *Courtesy of www.zapptoys.com* $15-16 MIP

Along with the decks, Expansion Sets of 64 cards each provide additional cards for players (trainers) to choose from. The Jungle Expansion Set was first released in the U.S. in July 1999. The Fossil Expansion Set (not yet available at the time of this writing) was released in November 1999.

To assist trainers in collecting every Pokémon, Booster Packs of eleven cards each are also available. Expansion Sets and Booster Packs provide game players and collectors greater opportunities to collect the uncommon and rare Pokémon cards. Players frequently trade among themselves as well, swapping Pokémon monsters they have in abundance for others they have yet to acquire. This trading is, in fact, one of the more popular aspects of the Pokémon game.

Eleven card Jungle Booster Pack by Wizards of the Coast. Featured here is a rare Flareon holographic foil trading card, $11-12; $15-16 Edition 1. The first price listing is for the unlimited printing of the card, which followed closely on the heels of the first edition printing.

THE CARDS

Players and collectors alike share the goal of collecting all of the Pokémon cards. In America, 150 different Pokémon creatures became available for the first time with the introduction of the Fossil Expansion Set. As previously stated, some cards are much easier to come by than others. Most of the Energy cards (Grass, Fire, Water, Lightning, Psychic, and Fighting) are fairly common. However, the Colorless Energy card is harder to come by. Pokémon, Evolution, and Trainer cards range from common, to uncommon, to rare. The rarest of the bunch are the cards printed with holographic foil backgrounds.

For parents: no doubt you have been in the situation where your child holds up a Pokémon card to you and exclaims "This card is rare!" When you have asked how your offspring has come by this information, he or she cryptically replies "It's printed right on the card. See?"

Machamp Holographic Foil Trading Card, Evolution Stage 2, Edition 1, Base Set: LV. 67, #68, 8/102, Rare. *Courtesy of the Michael W. Snyder Collection.* $9-10; $10-11 Edition 1.

The card is then waved in your face and the child leaves the room with a superior grin, certain that you don't have a clue. Here is the secret. To determine if a card is common, uncommon, or rare, carefully examine its lower right hand corner. There you will find a small black circle, diamond or star. Common cards are marked with the circle, uncommon cards with the diamond, and rare cards with the star. (Gutschera 1998, 3)

First edition cards are also marked with an "Edition 1" stamp. This is located just below the lower left hand corner of the image of the Pokémon on the card. It consists of the word Edition wrapped around the upper half of a circle. Within the circle is the number one. When these cards are printed again in later editions, the symbol is removed, increasing the collectibility of Edition 1 cards.

There are several Pokémon card types. The Basic Pokémon cards provide the first creatures used to battle your opponents. Evolution cards represent "evolved" forms of the basic Pokémon, larger and stronger combatants. Energy cards are attached to the Pokémon, giving them their power to engage in combat. Trainer cards add spice to the game, providing one time only chances to perform special feats during the game. (Gutschera 1998, 5)

The evolution of one Pokémon monster from its basic to its most advanced form.
Machop Trading Card, Basic Pokémon, Base Set: LV. 20, #66, 52/102, Common. *Courtesy of the Michael W. Snyder Collection.* $1-2
Machoke Trading Card, Evolution Stage 1, Base Set: LV. 40, #67, 34/102, Uncommon. *Courtesy of the Michael W. Snyder Collection.* $1-2
Machamp Holographic Foil Trading Card, Evolution Stage 2, Edition 1, Base Set: LV. 67, #68, 8/102, Rare. *Courtesy of the Michael W. Snyder Collection.* $9-10; $10-11 Edition 1.

All of the basic elements common to Pokémon trading cards are found on this Pikachu card. Pikachu Trading Card, Basic Pokémon, Base Set: LV. 12, #25, 58/102, Common. *Courtesy of the Michael W. Snyder Collection.* $0.60-0.65

Each Pokémon card is organized in the following order. At the top of each card are the Pokémon's name, its evolution stage, hit points and Pokémon type (the energy source it uses in combat). In the center of the cards, below the image of that Pokémon, are its special powers, data, attack cost and text, attack damage and flavor text. Along the very bottom edge of the card are the illustrator's name, the Pokémon's level, monster number, card number and rarity symbol. (Gutschera 1998, 7; Brokaw, et al. 1999, 21) Trainer and Energy cards have a similar, if simpler, layout.

In the captions you will find some of this information used to identify each card. Included in the captions are the Pokémon's name, evolution stage, set designation (whether that card is part of the Basic or Jungle set), level, monster number, and card number. Also included are value estimates for each card. Please remember that these values are estimates only and are not intended to be used to set card prices. In the end, any collectible is only worth what the buyer is willing to pay for it.

CARD SETS AND VALUES

BASE SET CARDS AND VALUES

The Base Set, containing 102 cards, was released in its first edition in January 1999. The unlimited print run quickly followed in February 1999. (Brokaw, et al. 1999, 9)

NAME	STATUS		Edition 1	Unlimited Print Run
1. Alakazam	Rare	Holographic	$22-24	$14-15
2. Blastoise	Rare	Holographic	$40-44	$20-22
3. Chansey	Rare	Holographic	$20-22	$14-15
4. Charizard	Rare	Holographic	$80-90	$35-40
5. Clefairy	Rare	Holographic	$22-24	$12-13
6. Gyarados	Rare	Holographic	$20-22	$14-15
7. Hitmonchan	Rare	Holographic	$20-22	$14-15
8. Machamp	Rare	Holographic	$10-11	$9-10
9. Magneton	Rare	Holographic	$15-16	$11-12
10. Mewtwo	Rare	Holographic	$20-22	$14-15
11. Nidoking	Rare	Holographic	$20-22	$12-13
12. Ninetales	Rare	Holographic	$22-24	$12-13
13. Poliwrath	Rare	Holographic	$24-26	$12-13
14. Raichu	Rare	Holographic	$24-26	$17-19
15. Venusaur	Rare	Holographic	$24-26	$15-16
16. Zapdos	Rare	Holographic	$24-26	$15-16
17. Beedrill	Rare			$6-7
18. Dragonair	Rare			$6-7
19. Dugtrio	Rare			$5-6
20. Electrabuzz	Rare			$8-9
21. Electrode	Rare			$5-6
22. Pigeotto	Rare			$6-7
23. Arcanine	Uncommon			$2-3
24. Charmeleon	Uncommon			$2-3
25. Dewgong	Uncommon			$1-2
26. Dratini	Uncommon			$1-2
27. Farfetch'd	Uncommon			$3-4
28. Growlithe	Uncommon			$1-2
29. Haunter	Uncommon			$1-2
30. Ivysaur	Uncommon			$1-2
31. Jynx	Uncommon			$1-2
32. Kadabra	Uncommon			$1-2
33. Kakuna	Uncommon			$1-2
34. Machoke	Uncommon			$1-2
35. Magikarp	Uncommon			$1-2
36. Magmar	Uncommon			$1-2
37. Nidorino	Uncommon			$1-2
38. Poliwhirl	Uncommon			$1-2
39. Porygon	Uncommon			$1-2
40. Raticate	Uncommon			$1-2
41. Seel	Uncommon			$1-2
42. Wartortle	Uncommon			$2-3
43. Abra	Common			$0.35-0.40
44. Bulbasaur	Common			$0.35-0.40
45. Caterpie	Common			$0.35-0.40
46. Charmander	Common			$0.35-0.40
47. Diglett	Common			$0.35-0.40
48. Doduo	Common			$0.35-0.40

NAME	STATUS	Unlimited Print Run
49. Drowzee	Common	$0.35-0.40
50. Gastly	Common	$0.35-0.40
51. Koffing	Common	$0.35-0.40
52. Machop	Common	$1-2
53. Magnemite	Common	$0.35-0.40
54. Metapod	Common	$0.35-0.40
55. Nidoran	Common	$0.35-0.40
56. Onix	Common	$0.35-0.40
57. Pidgey	Common	$0.35-0.40
58. Pikachu	Common	$0.60-0.65
59. Poliwag	Common	$0.35-0.40
60. Ponyta	Common	$0.35-0.40
61. Rattata	Common	$0.35-0.40
62. Sandshrew	Common	$0.35-0.40
63. Squirtle	Common	$0.35-0.40
64. Starmie	Common	$0.35-0.40
65. Staryu	Common	$0.35-0.40
66. Tangela	Common	$0.35-0.40
67. Voltorb	Common	$0.35-0.40
68. Vulpix	Common	$0.35-0.40
69. Weedle	Common	$0.35-0.40
70. Clefairy Doll	Rare	$2.75-3.25
71. Computer Search	Rare	$5-6
72. Devolution Spray	Rare	$2.75-3.25
73. Impostor Professor Oak	Rare	$2.75-3.25
74. Item Finder	Rare	$5-6
75. Lass	Rare	$2.75-3.25
76. Pokémon Breeder	Rare	$5-6
77. Pokémon Trader	Rare	$5-6
78. Scoop Up	Rare	$3.75-4.25
79. Super Energy Removal	Rare	$5-6
80. Defender	Uncommon	$1-2
81. Energy Retrieval	Uncommon	$1-2
82. Full Heal	Uncommon	$1-2
83. Maintenance	Uncommon	$1-2
84. PlusPower	Uncommon	$1-2
85. Pokémon Center	Uncommon	$1-2
86. Pokémon Flute	Uncommon	$1-2
87. Pokedex	Uncommon	$1-2
88. Professor Oak	Uncommon	$2-3
89. Revive	Uncommon	$1-2
90. Super Potion	Uncommon	$1-2
91. Bill	Common	$0.70-0.80
92. Energy Removal	Common	$0.70-0.80
93. Gust of Wind	Common	$0.60-0.65
94. Potion	Common	$0.60-0.65
95. Switch	Common	$0.60-0.65
96. Double Colorless Energy	Uncommon	$2-3
97. Fighting Energy		$0.50-0.55
98. Fire Energy		$0.50-0.55
99. Grass Energy		$0.50-0.55
100. Lightning Energy		$0.50-0.55
101. Psychic Energy		$0.50-0.55
102. Water Energy		$0.50-0.55

COLORLESS

The trading cards are arranged by their decks first (either the Base or Jungle Set). They are further organized, divided up under their energy type first (Colorless, Fighting, Fire, Grass, Lightning, Psychic, and Water). The cards are grouped together, showing the Basic Pokémon and its evolved forms. The cards are further arranged alphabetically, based on the name of the Basic Pokémon whenever possible.

All of the cards from the Basic, Jungle, and Fossil sets are listed in the text. Almost all of the available Pokémon from the Base and Jungle sets had been captured in photos when this book was written. The Fossil Expansion Set, unfortunately, was still months away from release when this book went to press. However, here is a really good sampling of the available cards. The rest *will* be captured and presented in future printings of this guide!

Chansey Holographic Foil Trading Card, Basic Pokémon, Base Set: LV. 55, #113, 3/102, Rare. *Courtesy of the Michael W. Snyder Collection.* $14-15; $20-22 Edition 1

Above: To show you this dynamic duo, cards from both the Base and Jungle sets had to be put together. Doduo Trading Card, Basic Pokémon, Base Set: LV. 10, #84, 48/102, Common. *Courtesy of the Michael W. Snyder Collection.* $0.35-0.40 Dodrio Trading Card, Evolution Stage 1, Edition 1, Jungle: LV. 28, #85, 34/64, Uncommon. *Courtesy of the Michael W. Snyder Collection.* $1-2

Right: Doduo Trading Card, Basic Pokémon, Base Set: LV. 10, #84, 48/102, Common. *Courtesy of the Michael W. Snyder Collection.* $0.35-0.40

Dratini Trading Card, Basic Pokémon, Base Set: LV. 10, #147, 26/102, Uncommon. *Courtesy of the Michael W. Snyder Collection.* $1-2

Above: Dragonair Trading Card, Evolution Stage 1, Base Set: LV. 33, #148, 18/102, Uncommon. *Courtesy of the Michael W. Snyder Collection.* $6-7

Left: Farfetch'd Trading Card, Basic Pokémon, Base Set: LV. 20, #83, 27/102, Uncommon. *Courtesy of the Michael W. Snyder Collection.* $3-4

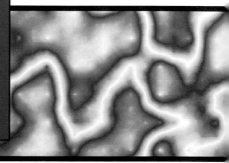

Pidgeotto Trading Card, Evolution Stage 1, Base Set: LV. 36, #17, 22/102, Rare. *Courtesy of www.zapptoys.com* $6-7

Above: Pidgey Trading Card, Basic Pokémon, Base Set: LV. 8, #16, 57/102, Common. *Courtesy of the Matthew Whiteford Collection.* $0.35-0.40

Left: Porygon Trading Card, Basic Pokémon, Base Set: LV. 12, #137, 39/102, Uncommon. *Courtesy of the Michael W. Snyder Collection.* $1-2

Rattata Trading Card, Basic Pokémon, Base Set: LV. 9, #19, 61/102, Common. *Courtesy of the Michael W. Snyder Collection.* $0.35-0.40

Raticate Trading Card, Evolution Stage 1, Base Set: LV. 41, #20, 40/102, Uncommon. *Courtesy of the Michael W. Snyder Collection.* $1-2

FIGHTING

Fighting Energy Trading Card, Base Set: 97/102. *Courtesy of the Michael W. Snyder Collection.* $0.50-0.55

Above: Diglett Trading Card, Basic Pokémon, Base Set: LV. 8, #50, 47/102, Common. *Courtesy of the Michael W. Snyder Collection.* $0.35-0.40

Left: Dugtrio Trading Card, Evolution Stage 1, Base Set: LV. 36, #51, 19/102, Common. *Courtesy of the Michael W. Snyder Collection.* $5-6

Machop Trading Card, Basic Pokémon, Base Set: LV. 20, #66, 52/102, Common. *Courtesy of the Michael W. Snyder Collection.* $1-2

Above: Machoke Trading Card, Evolution Stage 1, Base Set: LV. 40, #67, 34/102, Uncommon. *Courtesy of the Michael W. Snyder Collection.* $1-2

Right: Machamp Holographic Foil Trading Card, Evolution Stage 2, Edition 1, Base Set: LV. 67, #68, 8/102, Rare. *Courtesy of the Michael W. Snyder Collection.* $9-10; $10-11 Edition 1

Onix Trading Card, Basic Pokémon, Base Set: LV. 12, #95, 56/102, Common. *Courtesy of the Michael W. Snyder Collection.* $0.35-0.40

Sandshrew Trading Card, Basic Pokémon, Base Set: LV. 12, #27, 62/102, Common. *Courtesy of the Michael W. Snyder Collection.* $0.35-0.40

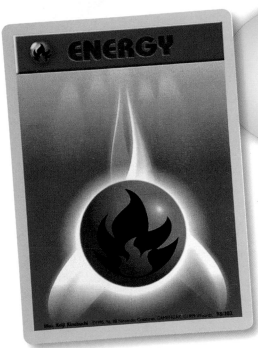

FIRE

Fire Energy
Trading Card,
Base Set: 98/102.
*Courtesy of the
Michael W.
Snyder Collec-
tion.* $0.50-0.55

Charmander Trading Card, Basic
Pokémon, Base Set: LV. 10, #4, 46/102,
Common. *Courtesy of the Michael W.
Snyder Collection.* $0.35-0.40

Charmeleon Trading Card, Evolution
Stage 1, Base Set: LV. 32, #5, 24/102,
Uncommon. *Courtesy of the Michael W.
Snyder Collection.* $2-3

STAGE 2

Evolves from Charmeleon Put Charizard on the Stage 1 card

Charizard 120 HP

Flame Pokémon. Length: 5' 7", Weight: 200 lbs.

Pokémon Power: Energy Burn As often as you like during your turn *(before your attack)*, you may turn all Energy attached to Charizard into Energy for the rest of the turn. This power can't be used if Charizard is Asleep, Confused, or Paralyzed.

Fire Spin Discard 2 Energy cards attached to Charizard in order to use this attack. **100**

weakness	resistance	retreat cost
🔥	👊 -30	✦ ✦ ✦

Spits fire that is hot enough to melt boulders. Known to unintentionally cause forest fires. LV. 76 #6

Illus. Mitsuhiro Arita ©1995, 96, 98 Nintendo, Creatures, GAMEFREAK. ©1999 Wizards. 4/102 ★

Charizard Holographic Foil Trading Card, Evolution Stage 2, Base Set: LV. 76, #6, 4/102, Rare. *Courtesy of www.zapptoys.com* $35-40; $80-90 Edition 1

Growlithe Trading Card, Basic Pokémon, Base Set: LV. 18, #58, 28/102, Common. *Courtesy of the Michael W. Snyder Collection.* $1-2

Above: Arcanine Trading Card, Evolution Stage 1, Base Set: LV. 45, #59, 23/102, Uncommon. *Courtesy of the Matthew Whiteford Collection.* $2-3

Left: Magmar Trading Card, Basic Pokémon, Base Set: LV. 24, #126, 36/102, Uncommon. *Courtesy of the Michael W. Snyder Collection.* $1-2

Ponyta Trading Card, Basic Pokémon, Base Set: LV. 10, #77, 60/102, Common. *Courtesy of the Michael W. Snyder Collection.* $0.35-0.40

Rapidash Trading Card, Evolution Stage 1, Edition 1, Jungle Set: LV. 33, #78, 44/64, Uncommon. *Courtesy of the Adam Whiteford Collection.* $1-2

Vulpix Trading Card, Basic Pokémon, Base Set: LV. 11, #37, 68/102, Common. *Courtesy of the Adam Whiteford Collection.* $0.35-0.40

Ninetales Holographic Foil Trading Card, Evolution Stage 1, Base Set: LV. 32, #38, 12/102, Rare. *Courtesy of www.zapptoys.com* $12-13; $22-24 Edition 1

GRASS

Grass Energy Trading
Card, Base Set: 99/102.
*Courtesy of the Michael
W. Snyder Collection.*
$0.50-0.55

Bulbasaur Trading Card, Basic Pokémon,
Base Set: LV. 13, #1, 44/102, Common.
*Courtesy of the Michael W. Snyder
Collection.* $0.35-0.40

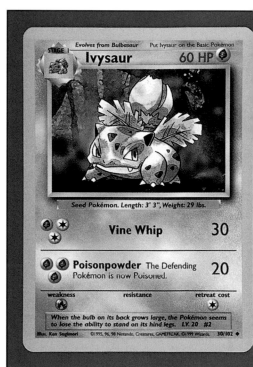

Ivysaur Trading Card, Evolution Stage 1,
Base Set: LV. 20, #2, 30/102, Common.
*Courtesy of the Michael W. Snyder
Collection.* $1-2

Evolves from Ivysaur   Put Venusaur on the Stage 1 card

STAGE 2

Venusaur   100 HP

Seed Pokémon. Length: 6' 7", Weight: 221 lbs.

Pokémon Power: Energy Trans As often as you like during your turn *(before your attack)*, you may take 1 Energy card attached to 1 of your Pokémon and attach it to a different one. This power can't be used if Venusaur is Asleep, Confused, or Paralyzed.

Solarbeam   60

weakness	resistance	retreat cost

This plant blooms when it is absorbing solar energy. It stays on the move to seek sunlight. LV. 67 #3

Illus. Mitsuhiro Arita ©1995, 96, 98 Nintendo, Creatures, GAMEFREAK. ©1999 Wizards.   15/102 ★

Venusaur Holographic Foil Trading Card, Evolution Stage 2, Base Set: LV. 67, #3, 15/102, Rare. *Courtesy of www.zapptoys.com* $15-16; $24-26 Edition 1

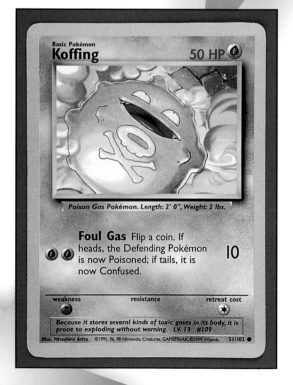

Above: Caterpie Trading Card, Basic Pokémon, Base Set: LV. 13, #10, 45/102, Common. *Courtesy of the Michael W. Snyder Collection.* $0.35-0.40 Metapod Trading Card, Evolution Stage 1, Base Set: LV. 21, #11, 54/102, Common. *Courtesy of the Michael W. Snyder Collection.* $0.35-0.40

Right: Koffing Trading Card, Basic Pokémon, Base Set: LV. 13, #109, 51/102, Common. *Courtesy of the Michael W. Snyder Collection.* $0.35-0.40

Basic Pokémon
Nidoran ♂ 40 HP

Poison Pin Pokémon. Length: 1' 4", Weight: 15 lbs.

Horn Hazard Flip a coin. If tails, this attack does nothing. **30**

weakness resistance retreat cost

Stiffens its ears to sense danger. The larger, more powerful of its horns secretes venom. LV. 20 #32

Illus. Ken Sugimori ©1995, 96, 98 Nintendo, Creatures, GAMEFREAK. ©1999 Wizards. 55/102 ●

Nidoran
Trading Card,
Basic Pokémon,
Base Set: LV.
20, #32, 55/
102, Common.
*Courtesy of the
Michael W.
Snyder
Collection.*
$0.35-0.40

STAGE 1 Evolves from Nidoran ♂ Put Nidorino on the Basic Pokémon
Nidorino 60 HP

Poison Pin Pokémon. Length: 2' 11", Weight: 43 lbs.

Double Kick Flip 2 coins. This attack does 30 damage times the number of heads. **30x**

Horn Drill **50**

weakness resistance retreat cost

An aggressive Pokémon that is quick to attack. The horn on its head secretes a powerful venom. LV. 25 #33

Illus. Mitsuhiro Arita ©1995, 96, 98 Nintendo, Creatures, GAMEFREAK. ©1999 Wizards. 37/102 ◆

Nidorino
Trading Card,
Evolution
Stage 1, Base
Set: LV. 25,
#33, 37/102,
Uncommon.
*Courtesy of
the Michael
W. Snyder
Collection.*
$1-2

STAGE 2

Evolves from Nidorino   Put Nidoking on the Stage 1 card

Nidoking   90 HP

Drill Pokémon. Length: 4' 7", Weight: 137 lbs.

Thrash Flip a coin. If heads, this attack does 30 damage plus 10 more damage; if tails, this attack does 30 damage and Nidoking does 10 damage to itself.   **30+**

Toxic The Defending Pokémon is now Poisoned. It now takes 20 Poison damage instead of 10 after each player's turn (*even if it was already Poisoned*).   **20**

weakness   resistance   retreat cost

Uses its powerful tail in battle to smash, constrict, then break its prey's bones.   LV. 48   #34

Illus. Ken Sugimori   ©1995, 96, 98 Nintendo. Creatures, GAMEFREAK. ©1999 Wizards.   11/102 ★

Nidoking Holographic Foil Trading Card, Evolution Stage 2, Base Set: LV. 48, #34, 11/102, Rare. *Courtesy of www.zapptoys.com* $12-13; $20-22 Edition 1

Tangela Trading Card, Basic Pokémon, Base Set: LV. 8, #114, 66/102, Common. *Courtesy of the Michael W. Snyder Collection.* $0.35-0.40

Weedle Trading Card, Basic Pokémon, Base Set: LV. 12, #13, 69/102, Common. *Courtesy of the Michael W. Snyder Collection.* $0.35-040

Kakuna Trading Card, Evolution Stage 1, Base Set: LV. 23, #14, 33/102, Uncommon. *Courtesy of the Michael W. Snyder Collection.* $1-2

STAGE 2

Evolves from Kakuna   Put Beedrill on the Stage 1 card

Beedrill   80 HP

Poison Bee Pokémon. Length: 3' 3", Weight: 65 lbs.

Twineedle Flip 2 coins. This attack does 30 damage times the number of heads.

30x

Poison Sting Flip a coin. If heads, the Defending Pokémon is now Poisoned.

40

weakness	resistance	retreat cost
🔥	👊 -30	

Flies at high speed and attacks using the large, venomous stingers on its forelegs and tail.   LV. 32   #15

Illus. Ken Sugimori   ©1995, 96, 98 Nintendo, Creatures, GAMEFREAK. ©1999 Wizards.   17/102 ★

Beedrill Trading Card, Evolution Stage 2, Base Set: LV. 32, #15, 17/102, Rare. *Courtesy of the Michael W. Snyder Collection.* $6-7

LIGHTNING

Lightning Energy
Trading Card, Base Set:
100/102. *Courtesy of
the Michael W. Snyder
Collection.* $0.50-0.55

Electrode Trading
Card, Evolution
Stage 1, Base
Set: LV. 40, #101,
21/102, Rare.
*Courtesy of
www.zapptoys.com*
$5-6

Basic Pokémon

Magnemite   40 HP ⚡

Magnet Pokémon. Length: 1' 0", Weight: 13 lbs.

⚡ **Thunder Wave** Flip a coin. If heads, the Defending Pokémon is now Paralyzed.   **10**

⚡✴ **Selfdestruct** Does 10 damage to each Pokémon on each player's Bench. *(Don't apply Weakness and Resistance for Benched Pokémon.)* Magnemite does 40 damage to itself.   **40**

weakness   resistance   retreat cost

Uses anti-gravity to stay suspended. Appears without warning and uses attacks like Thunder Wave. LV. 13 #81

Illus. Keiji Kinebuchi   ©1995, 96, 98 Nintendo, Creatures, GAMEFREAK. ©1999 Wizards.   53/102 ●

Magnemite Trading Card, Basic Pokémon, Base Set: LV. 13, #81, 53/102, Common. *Courtesy of the Michael W. Snyder Collection.* $0.60-0.65

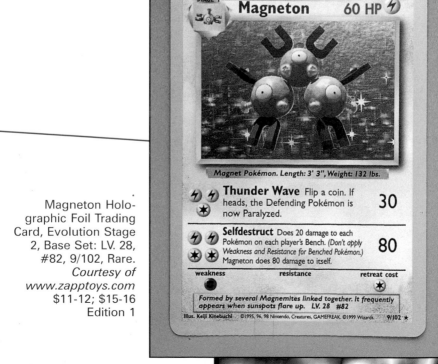

STAGE 1   *Evolves from Magnemite*   Put Magneton on the Basic Pokémon

Magneton   60 HP ⚡

Magnet Pokémon. Length: 3' 3", Weight: 132 lbs.

⚡⚡✴ **Thunder Wave** Flip a coin. If heads, the Defending Pokémon is now Paralyzed.   **30**

⚡⚡✴✴ **Selfdestruct** Does 20 damage to each Pokémon on each player's Bench. *(Don't apply Weakness and Resistance for Benched Pokémon.)* Magneton does 80 damage to itself.   **80**

weakness   resistance   retreat cost

Formed by several Magnemites linked together. It frequently appears when sunspots flare up. LV. 28 #82

Illus. Keiji Kinebuchi   ©1995, 96, 98 Nintendo, Creatures, GAMEFREAK. ©1999 Wizards.   9/102 ★

Magneton Holographic Foil Trading Card, Evolution Stage 2, Base Set: LV. 28, #82, 9/102, Rare. *Courtesy of www.zapptoys.com* $11-12; $15-16 Edition 1

Basic Pokémon
Pikachu   40 HP ⚡

Mouse Pokémon. Length: 1' 4", Weight: 13 lbs.

⭐ **Gnaw**   10

⚡⭐ **Thunder Jolt** Flip a coin. If tails,   30
Pikachu does 10 damage to itself.

weakness   resistance   retreat cost

*When several of these Pokémon gather, their electricity can
cause lightning storms. LV. 12 #25*

Illus. Mitsuhiro Arita © 1995, 96, 98, 99 Nintendo, Creatures, GAMEFREAK. © 1999 Wizards 58/102 ●

Left: Pikachu Trading Card, Basic Pokémon, Base Set: LV. 12, #25, 58/102, Common. *Courtesy of the Michael W. Snyder Collection.* $0.60-0.65

Below: Compare these two cards from the Base and Jungle sets and notice the differences between them. Pikachu Trading Card, Basic Pokémon, Base Set: LV. 12, #25, 58/102, Common. *Courtesy of the Michael W. Snyder Collection.* $0.60-0.65 Pikachu Trading Card, Basic Pokémon, Jungle: LV. 14, #25, 60/64, Common. *Courtesy of the Michael W. Snyder Collection.* $0.60-0.65

Basic Pokémon
Pikachu   40 HP ⚡

Mouse Pokémon. Length: 1' 4", Weight: 13 lbs.

⭐ **Gnaw**   10

⚡⭐ **Thunder Jolt** Flip a coin. If tails,   30
Pikachu does 10 damage to itself.

weakness   resistance   retreat cost

*When several of these Pokémon gather, their electricity can
cause lightning storms. LV. 12 #25*

Illus. Mitsuhiro Arita © 1995, 96, 98, 99 Nintendo, Creatures, GAMEFREAK. © 1999 Wizards 58/102 ●

Basic Pokémon
Pikachu   50 HP ⚡

Mouse Pokémon. Length: 1' 4", Weight: 13 lbs.

⚡⚡ **Spark** If your opponent has any
Benched Pokémon, choose 1 of   20
them and this attack does 10
damage to it. *(Don't apply Weakness
and Resistance for Benched Pokémon.)*

weakness   resistance   retreat cost

*When several of these Pokémon gather, their electricity can
build and cause lightning storms. LV. 14 #25*

Illus. Ken Sugimori ©1995, 96, 98 Nintendo, Creatures, GAMEFREAK. ©1999 Wizards 60/64 ●

Basic Pokémon
Zapdos

90 HP

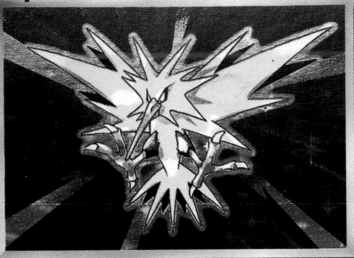

Electric Pokémon. Length: 5' 3", Weight: 116 lbs.

 Thunder Flip a coin. If tails, Zapdos does 30 damage to itself. **60**

 Thunderbolt Discard all Energy cards attached to Zapdos in order to use this attack. **100**

weakness	resistance	retreat cost
	⬛ -30	✦✦✦

A legendary bird Pokémon said to appear from clouds while wielding enormous lightning bolts. LV. 64 #145

Illus. Ken Sugimori · ©1995, 96, 98 Nintendo, Creatures, GAMEFREAK. ©1999 Wizards. 16/102 ★

PSYCHIC

Psychic Energy
Trading Card, Base
Set: 101/102 *Courtesy
of the Michael W.
Snyder Collection.*
$0.50-0.55

Abra Trading Card, Basic Pokémon, Base Set: LV. 10, #63, 43/102,
Common. *Courtesy of the Michael W. Snyder Collection.* $0.35-0.40
Kadabra Trading Card, Evolution Stage 1, Base Set: LV. 38, #64, 32/102,
Uncommon. *Courtesy of the Michael W. Snyder Collection.* $1-2

Alakazam Holographic Foil Trading Card, Evolution
Stage 2, Base Set: LV. 42, #65, 1/102, Rare. *Courtesy
of www.zapptoys.com* $14-15; $22-24 Edition 1

Drowzee Trading Card, Basic Pokémon, Base Set: LV. 12, #96, 49/102, Common. *Courtesy of the Michael W. Snyder Collection.* $0.35-0.40

Gastly Trading Card, Basic Pokémon, Base Set: LV. 8, #92, 50/102, Common. *Courtesy of the Michael W. Snyder Collection.* $0.35-0.40
Haunter Trading Card, Evolution Stage 1, Base Set: LV. 22, #93, 29/102, Uncommon. *Courtesy of the Michael W. Snyder Collection.* $1-2

Jynx Trading
Card, Basic
Pokémon, Base
Set: LV. 23, #124,
31/102, Uncommon. *Courtesy of
the Adam
Whiteford Collection.* $1-2

Mewtwo Holographic Foil Trading
Card, Basic
Pokémon, Base
Set: LV. 53, #150,
10/102, Rare.
*Courtesy of the
Matthew Whiteford
Collection.* $14-15;
$20-22 Edition 1

WATER

Water Energy Trading Card, Base Set: 102/102. *Courtesy of the Michael W. Snyder Collection.* $0.50-0.55

Magikarp Trading Card, Basic Pokémon, Base Set: LV. 8, #129, 35/102, Uncommon. *Courtesy of the Michael W. Snyder Collection.* $1-2

Gyarados Holographic Foil Trading Card, Evolution Stage 1, Base Set: LV. 41, #130, 6/102, Rare. *Courtesy of the Michael W. Snyder Collection.* $14-15; $20-22 Edition 1.

Poliwag Trading Card, Basic Pokémon, Base Set: LV. 13, #60, 59/102, Common. *Courtesy of the Michael W. Snyder Collection.* $0.35-0.40

Poliwhirl Trading Card, Evolution Stage 1, Base Set: LV. 28, #61, 38/102, Uncommon. *Courtesy of the Michael W. Snyder Collection.* $1-2

STAGE 2

Evolves from Poliwhirl — Put Poliwrath on the Stage 1 card

Poliwrath

90 HP

Tadpole Pokémon. Length: 4' 3", Weight: 119 lbs.

Water Gun Does 30 damage plus 10 more damage for each ⬤ Energy attached to Poliwrath but not used to pay for this attack's Energy cost. Extra ⬤ Energy after the 2nd doesn't count.

30+

Whirlpool If the Defending Pokémon has any Energy cards attached to it, choose 1 of them and discard it.

40

weakness	resistance	retreat cost
🌿		✦✦✦

An adept swimmer at both the front crawl and breaststroke. Easily overtakes the best human swimmers. LV. 48 #62

Illus. Ken Sugimori   ©1995, 96, 98 Nintendo, Creatures, GAMEFREAK. ©1999 Wizards.   13/102 ★

Poliwrath Holographic Foil Trading Card, Evolution Stage 2, Base Set: LV. 48, #62, 13/102, Rare. *Courtesy of the Michael W. Snyder Collection.* $12-13; $24-26 Edition 1.

Seel Trading Card, Basic Pokémon, Base Set: LV. 12, #86, 41/102, Uncommon. *Courtesy of www.zapptoys.com* $1-2

Dewgong Trading Card, Evolution Stage 1, Base Set: LV. 42, #87, 25/102, Uncommon. *Courtesy of www.zapptoys.com* $1-2

Squirtle Trading Card, Basic Pokémon, Base Set: LV. 8, #7, 63/102, Common. *Courtesy of the Michael W. Snyder Collection.* $0.35-0.40

Wartortle Trading Card, Evolution Stage 1, Base Set: LV. 22, #8, 42/102, Uncommon. *Courtesy of the Michael W. Snyder Collection.* $2-3

Right: Blastoise Holographic Foil Trading Card, Evolution Stage 2, Base Set: LV. 52, #9, 2/102, Rare. *Courtesy of www.zapptoys.com* $20-22; $40-44 Edition 1

Below: Staryu Trading Card, Basic Pokémon, Base Set: LV. 15, #120, 65/102, Common. *Courtesy of the Michael W. Snyder Collection.* $0.35-0.40
Starmie Trading Card, Evolution Stage 1, Base Set: LV. 28, #121, 64/102, Common. *Courtesy of the Michael W. Snyder Collection.* $0.35-0.40

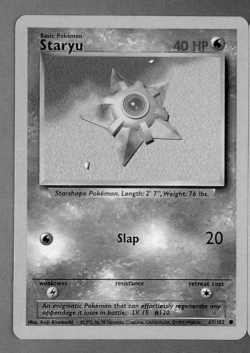

TRAINER

Clefairy Doll
10 HP

Play Clefairy Doll as if it were a Basic Pokémon. While in play, Clefairy Doll counts as a Pokémon (instead of a Trainer card). Clefairy Doll has no attacks, can't retreat, and can't be Asleep, Confused, Paralyzed, or Poisoned. If Clefairy Doll is Knocked Out, it doesn't count as a Knocked Out Pokémon. At any time during your turn before your attack, you may discard Clefairy Doll.

Illus. Keiji Kinebuchi © 1995, 96, 98, 99 Nintendo, Creatures, GAMEFREAK. © 1999 Wizards. 70/102 ★

TRAINERS

Clefairy Doll Trainer Trading Card, Base Set: 70/102, Rare. *Courtesy of www.zapptoys.com* $2.75-3.25

Computer Search Trainer Trading Card, Base Set: 71/102, Rare. *Courtesy of the Matthew Whiteford Collection.* $5-6

TRAINER

Computer Search

Discard 2 of the other cards from your hand in order to search your deck for any card and put it into your hand. Shuffle your deck afterward.

Illus. Keiji Kinebuchi © 1995, 96, 98 Nintendo, Creatures, GAMEFREAK. © 1999 Wizards. 71/102 ★

TRAINER

Devolution Spray

Choose 1 of your own Pokémon in play and a Stage of Evolution. Discard all Evolution cards of that Stage or higher attached to that Pokémon. That Pokémon is no longer Asleep, Confused, Paralyzed, Poisoned, or anything else that might be the result of an attack (just as if you had evolved it).

Illus. Keiji Kinebuchi   ©1995, 96, 98 Nintendo, Creatures, GAMEFREAK, ©1999 Wizards.   72/102 ★

Devolution Spray
Trainer Trading Card,
Base Set: 72/102,
Rare. *Courtesy of the
Michael W. Snyder
Collection.* $2.75-3.25

TRAINER

Impostor Professor Oak

Your opponent shuffles his or her hand into his or her deck, then draws 7 cards.

Illus. Ken Sugimori   © 1995, 96, 98, 99 Nintendo, Creatures, GAMEFREAK, © 1999 Wizards.   73/102 ★

Impostor Professor Oak
Trainer Trading Card,
Base Set: 73/102, Rare.
*Courtesy of
www.zapptoys.com*
$2.75-3.25

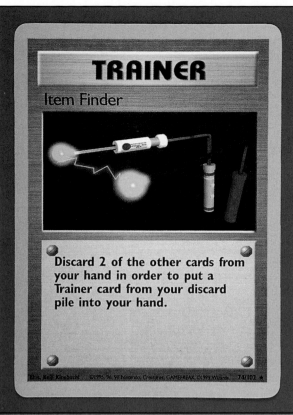

TRAINER

Item Finder

Discard 2 of the other cards from your hand in order to put a Trainer card from your discard pile into your hand.

Illus. Keiji Kinebuchi   ©1995, 96, 98 Nintendo, Creatures, GAMEFREAK. ©1999 Wizards.   74/102 ★

Item Finder Trainer Trading Card, Base Set: 74/102, Rare. *Courtesy of the Michael W. Snyder Collection.* $5-6

TRAINER

Lass

You and your opponent show each other your hands, then shuffle all the Trainer cards from your hands into your decks.

Illus. Ken Sugimori   © 1995, 96, 98, 99 Nintendo, Creatures, GAMEFREAK. © 1999 Wizards.   75/102 ★

Lass Trainer Trading Card, Base Set: 75/102, Rare. *Courtesy of www.zapptoys.com* $2.75-3.25

TRAINER

Pokémon Breeder

Put a Stage 2 Evolution card from your hand on the matching Basic Pokémon. You can only play this card when you would be allowed to evolve that Pokémon anyway.

Illus. Ken Sugimori   ©1995, 96, 98 Nintendo, Creatures, GAMEFREAK ©1999 Wizards.   76/102 ★

Pokémon Breeder Trainer Trading Card, Base Set: 76/102, Rare. *Courtesy of www.zapptoys.com* $5-6

TRAINER

Super Energy Removal

Discard 1 Energy card attached to 1 of your own Pokémon in order to choose 1 of your opponent's Pokémon and up to 2 Energy cards attached to it. Discard those Energy cards.

Illus. Keiji Kinebuchi   ©1995, 96, 98 Nintendo, Creatures, GAMEFREAK ©1999 Wizards.   79/102 ★

Super Energy Removal Trainer Trading Card: 79/102, Rare. *Courtesy of the Michael W. Snyder Collection.* $5-6

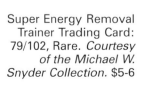

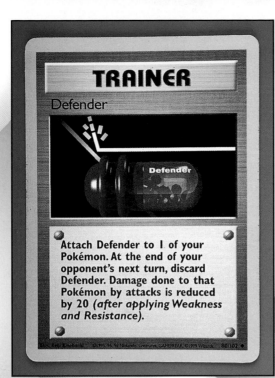

TRAINER

Defender

Attach Defender to 1 of your Pokémon. At the end of your opponent's next turn, discard Defender. Damage done to that Pokémon by attacks is reduced by 20 *(after applying Weakness and Resistance).*

Illus. Keiji Kinebuchi ©1995. 96, 98 Nintendo, Creatures, GAMEFREAK. ©1999 Wizards 80/102 ◆

Defender Trainer Trading Card, Base Set: 80/102, Uncommon. *Courtesy of the Matthew Whiteford Collection.* $1-2

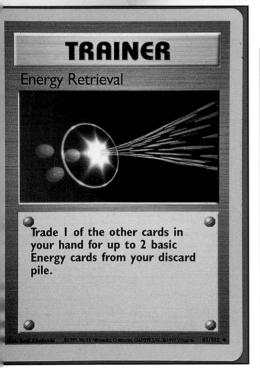

TRAINER

Energy Retrieval

Trade 1 of the other cards in your hand for up to 2 basic Energy cards from your discard pile.

Illus. Keiji Kinebuchi ©1995. 96, 98 Nintendo, Creatures, GAMEFREAK. ©1999 Wizards 81/102 ◆

Energy Retrieval Trainer Trading Card: 81/102, Rare. *Courtesy of the Michael W. Snyder Collection.* $1-2

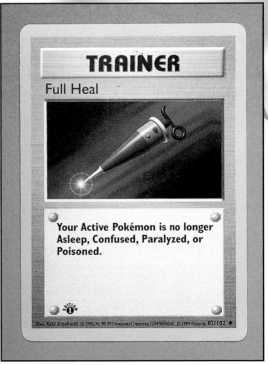

TRAINER

Full Heal

Your Active Pokémon is no longer Asleep, Confused, Paralyzed, or Poisoned.

Illus. Keiji Kinebuchi © 1995. 96, 98, 99 Nintendo, Creatures, GAMEFREAK. © 1999 Wizards 82/102 ◆

Full Heal Trainer Trading Card, Edition 1, Base Set: 82/102, Uncommon. *Courtesy of www.zapptoys.com* $1-2

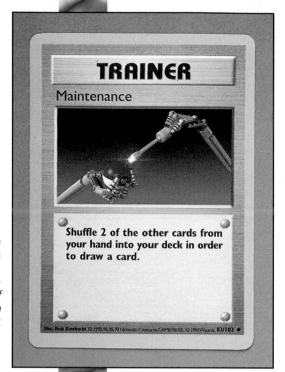

Maintenance Trainer Trading Card, Base Set: 83/102, Uncommon. *Courtesy of www.zapptoys.com* $1-2

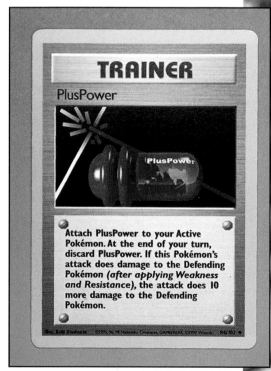

PlusPower Trainer Trading Card, Base Set: 84/102, Uncommon. *Courtesy of www.zapptoys.com* $1-2

Pokémon Center Trainer Trading Card, Base Set: 85/102, Uncommon. *Courtesy of www.zapptoys.com* $1-2

TRAINER

Pokémon Flute

Choose 1 Basic Pokémon card from your opponent's discard pile and put it onto his or her Bench. *(You can't play Pokémon Flute if your opponent's Bench is full.)*

Illus. Keiji Kinebuchi ©1995, 96, 98 Nintendo, Creatures, GAMEFREAK. ©1999 Wizards. 86/102

TRAINER

Pokédex

Look at up to 5 cards from the top of your deck and rearrange them as you like.

Illus. Keiji Kinebuchi ©1995, 96, 98 Nintendo, Creatures, GAMEFREAK. ©1999 Wizards. 87/102

TRAINER

Professor Oak

Discard your hand, then draw 7 cards.

Illus. Ken Sugimori ©1995, 96, 98 Nintendo, Creatures, GAMEFREAK. ©1999 Wizards. 88/102

Above: Pokémon Flute Trainer Trading Card: 86/102, Uncommon. *Courtesy of the Michael W. Snyder Collection.* $1-2
Pokedex Trainer Trading Card: 87/102, Uncommon. *Courtesy of the Michael W. Snyder Collection.* $1-2

Left: Professor Oak Trainer Trading Card, Base Set: 88/102, Common. *Courtesy of the Matthew Whiteford Collection.* $2-3

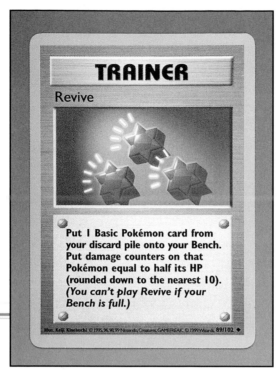

TRAINER

Revive

Put 1 Basic Pokémon card from your discard pile onto your Bench. Put damage counters on that Pokémon equal to half its HP (rounded down to the nearest 10). *(You can't play Revive if your Bench is full.)*

Illus. Keiji Kinebuchi © 1995, 96, 98,99 Nintendo, Creatures, GAMEFREAK. © 1999 Wizards. 89/102 ◆

Revive Trainer Trading Card, Base Set: 89/102, Uncommon. *Courtesy of www.zapptoys.com* $1-2

TRAINE

Super Potion

Discard 1 Energy card a
to 1 of your own Pokém
order to remove up to
counters from that Poké

Illus. Keiji Kinebuchi ©1995, 96, 98 Nintendo, Creatures, GAMEFREA

TRAINER

Gust of Wind

Choose 1 of your opponent's Benched Pokémon and switch it with his or her Active Pokémon.

Illus. Keiji Kinebuchi ©1995, 96, 98 Nintendo, Creatures, GAMEFREAK. ©1999 Wizards. 93/102 ■

TRAINER

Potion

Remove up to 2 damage counters from 1 of your Pokémon.

Illus. Keiji Kinebuchi ©1995, 96, 98 Nintendo, Creatures, GAMEFREAK. ©1999 Wizards. 94/102 ■

TRAINER

Bill

Draw 2 cards.

Illus. Ken Sugimori   ©1995, 96, 98 Nintendo, Creatures, GAMEFREAK. ©1999 Wizards.   91/102

TRAINER

Energy Removal

Choose 1 Energy card attached to
1 of your opponent's Pokémon
and discard it.

Illus. Keiji Kinebuchi   ©1995, 96, 98 Nintendo, Creatures, GAMEFREAK. ©1999 Wizards.   92/102

TRAINER

h 1 of your Benched
non with your Active
non.

©1995, 96, 98 Nintendo, Creatures, GAMEFREAK. ©1999 Wizards.   95/102

Above: Super Potion Trainer
Trading Card, Base Set: 90/102,
Uncommon. *Courtesy of the
Michael W. Snyder Collection.* $1-2
Bill Trainer Trading Card, Base Set:
91/102, Common. *Courtesy of the
Michael W. Snyder Collection.*
$0.70-0.80
Energy Removal Trainer Trading
Card, Base Set: 92/102, Common.
*Courtesy of the Michael W. Snyder
Collection.* $0.70-0.80

Left: Gust of Wind Trainer Trading
Card, Base Set: 93/102, Common.
*Courtesy of the Michael W. Snyder
Collection.* $0.60-0.65
Potion Trainer Trading Card, Base
Set: 94/102, Common. *Courtesy of
the Michael W. Snyder Collection.*
$0.60-0.65
Switch Trainer Trading Card, Base
Set: 95/102, Common. *Courtesy of
the Michael W. Snyder Collection.*
$0.60-0.65

JUNGLE EXPANSION SET AND VALUES

The Jungle Expansion Set, containing 64 cards, was released in its first edition in June 1999. The unlimited print run began in July 1999. (Brokaw, et al. 1999, 12)

Name	Status		Edition 1	Unlimited Print Run
1. Clefable	Rare	Holographic	$14-15	$10-11
2. Electrode	Rare	Holographic	$14-15	$8-9
3. Flareon	Rare	Holographic	$15-16	$11-12
4. Jolteon	Rare	Holographic	$16-18	$11-12
5. Kangaskhan	Rare	Holographic	$14-15	$9-10
6. Mr. Mime	Rare	Holographic	$13-14	$8-9
7. Nidoqueen	Rare	Holographic	$12-13	$8-9
8. Pidgeot	Rare	Holographic	$13-14	$8-9
9. Pinsir	Rare	Holographic	$12-13	$7-8
10. Scyther	Rare	Holographic	$16-18	$11-12
11. Snorlax	Rare	Holographic	$14-15	$11-12
12. Vaporeon	Rare	Holographic	$15-16	$11-12
13. Venomoth	Rare	Holographic	$14-15	$9-10
14. Victreebel	Rare	Holographic	$13-14	$8-9
15. Vileplume	Rare	Holographic	$12-13	$10-11
16. Wigglytuff	Rare	Holographic	$15-16	$10-11
17. Clefable	Rare			$6-7
18. Electrode	Rare			$5-6
19. Flareon	Rare			$6-7
20. Jolteon	Rare			$6-7
21. Kangaskhan	Rare			$4-5
22. Mr. Mime	Rare			$4-5
23. Nidoqueen	Rare			$5-6
24. Pidgeot	Rare			$5-6
25. Pinsir	Rare			$5-6
26. Scyther	Rare			$5-6
27. Snorlax	Rare			$5-6
28. Vaporeon	Rare			$6-7
29. Venomoth	Rare			$4-5
30. Victreebel	Rare			$4-5
31. Vileplume	Rare			$5-6
32. Wigglytuff	Rare			$5-6

Name	Status	Unlimited Print Run
33. Butterfree	Uncommon	$1-2
34. Dodrio	Uncommon	$1-2
35. Exeggutor	Uncommon	$1-2
36. Fearow	Uncommon	$1-2
37. Gloom	Uncommon	$1-2
38. Lickitung	Uncommon	$1-2
39. Marowak	Uncommon	$1-2
40. Nidorina	Uncommon	$1-2
41. Parasect	Uncommon	$1-2
42. Persian	Uncommon	$1-2
43. Primeape	Uncommon	$1-2
44. Rapidash	Uncommon	$1-2
45. Rhydon	Uncommon	$1-2
46. Seaking	Uncommon	$1-2
47. Tauros	Uncommon	$1-2
48. Weepinbell	Uncommon	$1-2
49. Bellsprout	Common	$0.60-0.65
50. Cubone	Common	$0.60-0.65
51. Eevee	Common	$0.60-0.65
52. Exeggcute	Common	$0.60-0.65
53. Goldeen	Common	$0.30-0.35
54. Jigglypuff	Common	$0.80-0.90
55. Mankey	Common	$0.60-0.65
56. Meowth	Common	$0.30-0.35
57. Nidoran	Common	$0.60-0.65
58. Oddish	Common	$0.60-0.65
59. Paras	Common	$0.30-0.35
60. Pikachu	Common	$0.60-0.65
61. Rhyhorn	Common	$0.60-0.65
62. Spearow	Common	$0.80-0.90
63. Venonat	Common	$0.30-0.35
64. Poké Ball	Common	$0.30-0.35

Note: Cards 1-16 are holographic versions of cards 17-32. Otherwise, these cards are exactly the same as their non-holo versions.

COLORLESS

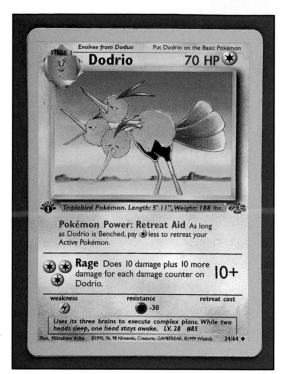

Dodrio Trading Card, Evolution Stage 1, Edition 1, Jungle: LV. 28, #85, 34/64, Uncommon. *Courtesy of the Michael W. Snyder Collection.* $1-2

Eevee Trading Card, Basic Pokémon, Edition 1, Jungle: LV. 12, #133, 51/64, Common. *Courtesy of the Michael W. Snyder Collection.* $0.60-0.65
One of Eevee's several evolved forms, using a different energy type. Flareon Trading Card, Evolution Stage 1, Jungle: LV. 28, #136, 3/64, Rare. *Courtesy of the Michael W. Snyder Collection.* $11-12; $15-16 Edition 1

Jigglypuff Trading Card, Basic Pokémon, Edition 1, Jungle: LV. 14, #39, 54/64, Common. *Courtesy of the Michael W. Snyder Collection.* $0.80-0.90

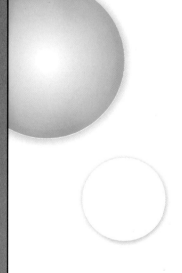

Wigglytuff Trading Card, Evolution Stage 1, Jungle: LV. 36, #40, 32/64, Rare. *Courtesy of www.zapptoys.com* $5-6

74

Kangaskhan Holographic Foil Trading Card, Basic Pokémon, Jungle: LV. 40, #115, 5/64, Rare. *Courtesy of www.zapptoys.com* $9-10; $14-15 Edition 1

Kangaskhan Trading Card, Basic Pokémon, Jungle: LV. 40, #115, 21/64, Rare. *Courtesy of www.zapptoys.com* $4-5

Basic Pokémon
Lickitung   90 HP

Licking Pokémon. Length: 3' 11", Weight: 144 lbs.

Tongue Wrap Flip a coin. If heads, the Defending Pokémon is now Paralyzed.   **10**

Supersonic Flip a coin. If heads, the Defending Pokémon is now Confused.

weakness   resistance -30   retreat cost

Its tongue can be extended like a chameleon's. It leaves a stinging sensation when it licks enemies. LV. 26 #108

Illus. Mitsuhiro Arita ©1995, 96, 98 Nintendo, Creatures, GAMEFREAK. ©1999 Wizards.   38/64

Lickitung Trading Card, Basic Pokémon, Jungle Set: LV. 26, #108, 38/64, Uncommon. *Courtesy of the Adam Whiteford Collection.* $1-2

Basic Pokémon
Meowth   50 HP

Scratch Cat Pokémon. Length: 1' 4", Weight: 9 lbs.

Pay Day Flip a coin. If heads, draw a card.   **10**

weakness   resistance -30   retreat cost

Adores circular objects. Wanders the streets on a nightly basis to look for dropped loose change. LV. 15 #52

Illus. Mitsuhiro Arita ©1995, 96, 98 Nintendo, Creatures, GAMEFREAK. ©1999 Wizards.   56/64

Meowth Trading Card, Basic Pokémon, Jungle: LV. 15, #52, 56/64, Common. *Courtesy of the Michael W. Snyder Collection.* $0.30-0.35

STAGE 1   *Evolves from Meowth*   Put Persian on the Basic Pokémon
Persian   70 HP

Classy Cat Pokémon. Length: 3' 3", Weight: 71 lbs.

Scratch   **20**

Pounce If the Defending Pokémon attacks Persian during your opponent's next turn, any damage done by the attack is reduced by 10 (after applying Weakness and Resistance). (Benching either Pokémon ends this effect.)   **30**

weakness   resistance -30   retreat cost

Although its fur has many admirers, it is tough to raise as a pet because of its fickle meanness. LV. 25 #53

Illus. Kagemaru Himeno ©1995, 96, 98 Nintendo, Creatures, GAMEFREAK. ©1999 Wizards.   42/64

Persian Trading Card, Evolution Stage 1, Jungle: LV. 25, #53, 42/64, Uncommon. *Courtesy of the Michael W. Snyder Collection.* $1-2

Spearow Trading Card, Basic Pokémon, Edition 1, Jungle: LV. 13, #21, 62/64, Common. *Courtesy of the Michael W. Snyder Collection.* $0.80-0.90

Fearow Trading Card, Evolution Stage 1, Jungle: LV. 27, #22, 36/64, Uncommon. *Courtesy of www.zapptoys.com* $1-2

Pidgeot Trading Card, Evolution Stage 2, Jungle: LV. 40, #18, 24/64, Rare. *Courtesy of www.zapptoys.com* $5-6

Tauros Trading Card, Basic Pokémon, Jungle: LV. 32, #128, 47/64, Uncommon. *Courtesy of www.zapptoys.com* $1-2

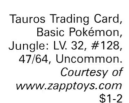

FIGHTING

Please note that the energy cards shown here are from the Base Set. They are very useful, however, for heading up each of the sections. Fighting Energy Trading Card, Base Set: 97/102. *Courtesy of the Michael W. Snyder Collection.* $0.50-0.55

Cubone Trading Card, Basic Pokémon, Edition 1, Jungle: LV. 13, #104, 50/64, Common. *Courtesy of the Michael W. Snyder Collection.* $0.60-0.65
Marowak Trading Card, Evolution Stage 1, Jungle: LV. 26, #105, 39/64, Uncommon. *Courtesy of the Michael W. Snyder Collection.* $1-2

Mankey Trading Card, Basic Pokémon, Jungle, LV. 7, #56, 55/64, Common. *Courtesy of the Michael W. Snyder Collection.* $0.60-0.65

Primeape Trading Card, Evolution Stage 1, Jungle: LV. 35, #57, 43/64, Uncommon. *Courtesy of www.zapptoys.com* $1-2

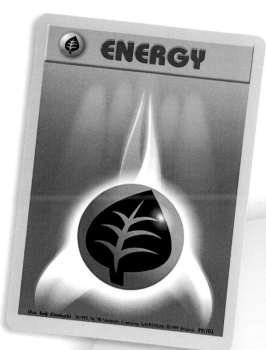

GRASS

Grass Energy Trading
Card, Base Set: 99/102.
*Courtesy of the Michael
W. Snyder Collection.*
$0.50-0.55

Bellsprout Trading Card, Basic Pokémon,
Edition 1, Jungle: LV. 11, #69, 49/64,
Common. *Courtesy of the Michael W.
Snyder Collection.* $0.60-0.65

Weepinbell Trading Card, Evolution
Stage 1, Jungle: LV. 28, #70, 48/64,
Uncommon. *Courtesy of the Michael
W. Snyder Collection.* $1-2

Victreebel Holographic Foil Trading Card, Evolution Stage 2, Jungle: LV. 42, #71, 14/64, Rare. *Courtesy of www.zapptoys.com* $8-9; $13-14 Edition 1

Victreebel Trading Card, Evolution Stage 2, Edition 1, Jungle: LV. 42, #71, 30/64, Rare. *Courtesy of the Michael W. Snyder Collection.* $4-5

Butterfree Trading Card, Evolution Stage 2, Jungle Set: LV. 28, #12, 33/64, Uncommon. *Courtesy of the Adam Whiteford Collection.* $1-2

Exeggcute Trading Card, Basic Pokémon, Jungle: LV. 14, #102, 52/64, Common. *Courtesy of the Michael W. Snyder Collection.* $0.60-0.65

Exeggutor Trading Card, Evolution Stage 1, Jungle: LV. 35, #103, 35/64, Uncommon. *Courtesy of www.zapptoys.com* $1-2

Nidoran Trading Card, Basic Pokémon, Jungle: LV. 13, #29, 57/64, Common. *Courtesy of the Michael W. Snyder Collection.* $0.60-0.65

Nidorina Trading Card, Evolution Stage 1, Jungle: LV. 24, #30, 40/64, Uncommon. *Courtesy of the Michael W. Snyder Collection.* $1-2

Nidoqueen Trading Card, Evolution Stage 2, Jungle: LV. 43, #31, 23/64, Rare. *Courtesy of www.zapptoys.com* $5-6

Nidoqueen Holographic Foil Trading Card, Evolution
Stage 2, Jungle: LV. 43, #31, 7/64, Rare. *Courtesy of
www.zapptoys.com* $8-9; $12-13 Edition 1

Oddish Trading Card, Basic Pokémon, Edition 1, Jungle: LV. 8, #43, 58/64, Common. *Courtesy of the Michael W. Snyder Collection.* $0.60-0.65

Vileplume Trading Card, Evolution Stage 2, Jungle: LV. 35, #45, 31/64, Rare. *Courtesy of the Michael W. Snyder Collection.* $5-6

Gloom Trading Card, Evolution Stage 1, Edition 1, Jungle: LV. 22, #44, 37/64, Uncommon. *Courtesy of the Michael W. Snyder Collection.* $1-2

Paras Trading Card,
Basic Pokémon, Jungle:
LV. 8, #46, 59/64,
Common. *Courtesy of
the Michael W. Snyder
Collection.* $0.30-0.35

Pinsir Holographic Foil
Trading Card, Basic
Pokémon, Jungle: LV. 24,
#127, 9/64, Rare. *Courtesy
of www.zapptoys.com* $7-8;
$12-13 Edition 1

Scyther Holographic Foil Trading Card, Basic Pokémon, Jungle: LV. 25, #123, 10/64, Rare. *Courtesy of www.zapptoys.com* $11-12; $16-18 Edition 1

Scyther Trading Card, Basic Pokémon, Jungle: LV. 25, #123, 26/64, Rare. *Courtesy of www.zapptoys.com* $5-6

Venonat Trading Card, Basic Pokémon, Edition 1, Jungle: LV. 12, #12, 63/64, Common. *Courtesy of the Michael W. Snyder Collection.* $0.30-0.40

Venomoth Trading Card, Evolution Stage 1, Jungle: LV. 28, #49, 29/64, Rare. *Courtesy of www.zapptoys.com* $4-5

STAGE 1

Evolves from Venonat   Put Venomoth on the Basic Pokémon

Venomoth   70 HP

Poisonmoth Pokémon. Length: 4' 11", Weight: 28 lbs.

Pokémon Power: Shift Once during your turn *(before your attack),* you may change the type of Venomoth to the type of any other Pokémon in play other than Colorless. This power can't be used if Venomoth is Asleep, Confused, or Paralyzed.

Venom Powder Flip a coin. If heads, the Defending Pokémon is now Confused and Poisoned.   10

weakness	resistance	retreat cost
	-30	

The dust-like scales covering its wings are color coded to indicate the kinds of poison it has. LV. 28 #49

Illus. Ken Sugimori   ©1995, 96, 98 Nintendo, Creatures, GAMEFREAK. ©1999 Wizards.   13/64 ★

LIGHTNING

Lightning Energy Trading Card, Base Set: 100/102. *Courtesy of the Michael W. Snyder Collection.* $0.50-0.55

Electrode Trading Card, Evolution Stage 1, Jungle: LV. 42, #101, 18/64, Rare. *Courtesy of www.zapptoys.com* $5-6

STAGE 1

Evolves from Voltorb   Put Electrode on the Basic Pokémon

Electrode

90 HP

Ball Pokémon. Length: 3' 11", Weight: 147 lbs.

 Tackle **20**

 Chain Lightning If the Defending Pokémon isn't Colorless, this attack does 10 damage to each Benched Pokémon of the same type as the Defending Pokémon *(including your own).* **20**

weakness	resistance	retreat cost
■		

It stores electrical energy under very high pressure. It often explodes with little or no provocation. **LV. 42 #101**

Illus. Mitsuhiro Arita   ©1995, 96, 98 Nintendo, Creatures, GAMEFREAK. ©1999 Wizards.   2/64 ★

Electrode Holographic Foil Trading Card, Evolution Stage 1, Jungle: LV. 42, #101, 2/64, Rare. *Courtesy of www.zapptoys.com* $8-9; $14-15 Edition 1

Jolteon Trading Card, Evolution Stage 1, Jungle: LV. 29, #135, 20/64, Rare. *Courtesy of www.zapptoys.com* $6-7

Pikachu Trading Card, Basic Pokémon, Jungle: LV. 14, #25, 60/64, Common. *Courtesy of the Michael W. Snyder Collection.* $0.60-0.65

Psychic Energy Trading Card, Base Set: 101/102 *Courtesy of the Michael W. Snyder Collection.* $0.50-0.55

Mr. Mime Holographic Foil Trading Card, Basic Pokémon, Jungle: LV. 28, #122, 6/64, Rare. *Courtesy of www.zapptoys.com* $8-9; $13-14 Edition

Mr. Mime Trading Card, Basic Pokémon, Jungle: LV. 28, #122, 22/64, Rare. *Courtesy of the Michael W. Snyder Collection.* $4-5

WATER

Water Energy
Trading Card, Base
Set: 102/102.
*Courtesy of the
Michael W. Snyder
Collection.* $0.50-0.55

Goldeen Trading Card, Basic
Pokémon, Jungle: LV. 12, #118,
53/64, Common. *Courtesy of the
Adam Whiteford Collection.*
$0.30-0.35

Seaking Trading Card, Evolution
Stage 1, Jungle: LV. 28, #119, 46/64,
Uncommon. *Courtesy of
www.zapptoys.com* $1-2

Vaporeon Holographic Foil Trading Card, Evolution Stage 1, Jungle: LV. 42, #134, 12/64, Rare. *Courtesy of www.zapptoys.com* $11-12; $15-16 Edition 1

Vaporeon Trading Card, Evolution Stage 1, Jungle: LV. 42, #134, 28/64, Rare. *Courtesy of www.zapptoys.com* $6-7

HAVE A BALL!

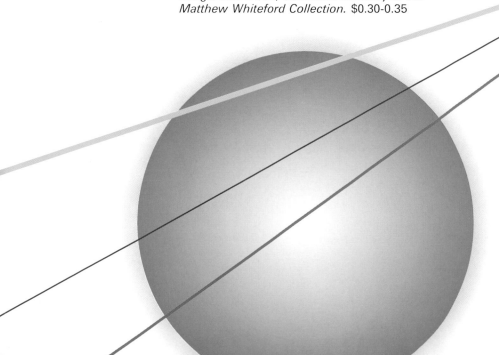

Poké Ball Trainer Trading Card, Edition 1,
Jungle Set: 64/64, Common. *Courtesy of the
Matthew Whiteford Collection.* $0.30-0.35

FOSSIL EXPANSION SET

The Fossil Expansion Set, not yet available at the time this book was written, is scheduled for release in America in November 1999 ... as is the movie. When the Fossil Expansion Set hits the market, 150 Pokémon monsters will be available for American trainers and collectors to catch. (Brokaw, et al. 1999, 14)

Name	Status			Edition 1	Unlimited Print Run
1. Aerodactyl	Rare	Holographic		CRP	CRP
2. Articuno	Rare	Holographic		CRP	CRP
3. Ditto	Rare	Holographic		CRP	CRP
4. Dragonite	Rare	Holographic		CRP	CRP
5. Gengar	Rare	Holographic		CRP	CRP
6. Haunter	Rare	Holographic		CRP	CRP
7. Hitmonlee	Rare	Holographic		CRP	CRP
8. Hypno	Rare	Holographic		CRP	CRP
9. Kabutops	Rare	Holographic		CRP	CRP
10. Lapras	Rare	Holographic		CRP	CRP
11. Magneton	Rare	Holographic		CRP	CRP
12. Moltres	Rare	Holographic		CRP	CRP
13. Muk	Rare	Holographic		CRP	CRP
14. Raichu	Rare	Holographic		CRP	CRP
15. Zapdos	Rare	Holographic		CRP	CRP
16. Aerodactyl	Rare				CRP
17. Articuno	Rare				CRP
18. Ditto	Rare				CRP
19. Dragonite	Rare				CRP
20. Gengar	Rare				CRP
21. Haunter	Rare				CRP
22. Hitmonlee	Rare				CRP
23. Hypno	Rare				CRP
24. Kabutops	Rare				CRP
25. Lapras	Rare				CRP
26. Magneton	Rare				CRP
27. Moltres	Rare				CRP
28. Muk	Rare				CRP
29. Raichu	Rare				CRP
30. Zapdos	Rare				CRP
31. Arbok	Uncommon				CRP
32. Cloyster	Uncommon				CRP
33. Gastly	Uncommon				CRP
34. Golbat	Uncommon				CRP
35. Golduck	Uncommon				CRP
36. Golem	Uncommon				CRP
37. Graveler	Uncommon				CRP
38. Kingler	Uncommon				CRP

Name	Status	Edition 1	Unlimited Print Run
39. Magmar	Uncommon		CRP
40. Omastar	Uncommon		CRP
41. Sandslash	Uncommon		CRP
42. Seadra	Uncommon		CRP
43. Slowbro	Uncommon		CRP
44. Tentacruel	Uncommon		CRP
45. Weezing	Uncommon		CRP
46. Ekans	Common		CRP
47. Geodude	Common		CRP
48. Grimer	Common		CRP
49. Horsea	Common		CRP
50. Kabuto	Common		CRP
51. Krabby	Common		CRP
52. Omanyte	Common		CRP
53. Psyduck	Common		CRP
54. Shellder	Common		CRP
55. Slowpoke	Common		CRP
56. Tentacool	Common		CRP
57. Zubat	Common		CRP
58. Old Man Fuji	Uncommon		CRP
59. Energy Transfer	Common		CRP
60. Gambler	Common		CRP
61. Recycle	Common		CRP
62. Mysterious Fossil	Common		CRP

At the time this was written, the Fossil deck cards were too new to have developed reliable secondary market (collector's) values. When this book is revised, and the Fossil cards have been on the market for a while, the Current Retail Price code (CRP) will be replaced with the prices collector's could expect to pay for these cards in mint condition if purchased from dealers or other collectors.

There are four Pokémon pre-constructed theme decks currently available for the Base Set and at least one set in the works for the Jungle Expansion Set. Each theme deck has different strengths to pit against opponents.

Also available to collectors, through import retailers and dealers, are the original Japanese Pocket Monster game decks, printed in Japanese. These are of interest as they include many cards which had yet to be released in America at the time of this writing. (Brokaw, et al. 1999, 136)

Pokémon card holders keep your cards neat, clean and ready for use. Kept like this, the cards will last longer than they would stuck in your pocket and they will retain their collector's value. *Courtesy of the Michael W. Snyder Collection.*

If you carry your Pokémon cards in your pocket, instead of protecting them in plastic sleeves of some sort, you might forget to take them out of your pants at the end of the day ... and you'll be sorry. This forgotten Arcanine card went through the washing machine. Arcanine Trading Card, Evolution Stage 1, Base Set: LV. 45, #59, 23/102, Uncommon. *Courtesy of the Michael W. Snyder Collection.* $2-3 (mint and unlaundered)

Other Pokémon Collectibles

Please note that many of these items have not yet been around in the United States long enough to have developed reliable secondary market values. In those cases, rather than guess which items will be truly rare and sought after by collectors in years to come—and possibly fail miserably as a predictor of future events, current retail prices (CRP) have been provided. When the book is updated, and reliable collector's values are available, these prices will be adjusted accordingly.

Comics

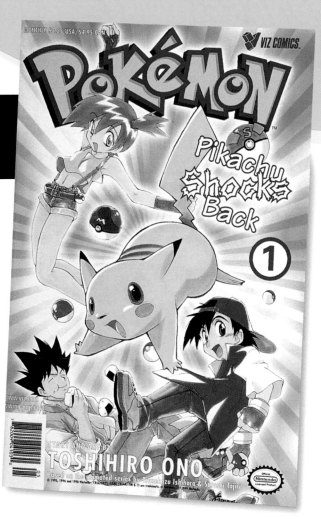

Pikachu Shocks Back #1 comic book by Viz Comics. $3-4 each CRP

There are several comic series to date by Viz Comics and the number is sure to grow. Available in America so far are:

The Electric Tale of Pikachu
 A four issue monthly series released from November 1998 - February 1999.
 $3-4 each CRP*
 (*Current Retail Price)

Pikachu Shocks Back
 A four issue monthly series released from March - June 1999.
 $3-4 each CRP
 Pikachu Shocks Back has also been released by Viz Comics as a graphic novel in November 1999. $13-14 CRP

Electric Pikachu Boogaloo
 A four issue monthly series released from July - October 1999.
 $3-4 each CRP

Pokémon Adventures, Issues #1-3
 #1. Mysterious Mew (introducing the rare 151st Pokémon, September 1999) $6-7 CRP
  #2. Wanted: Pikachu!
   (October 1999)
   $6-7 CRP
  #3. Starmie Surprise
   (November 1999)
   $6-7 CRP

Pokémon: Surf's Up, Pikachu!
 A four issue monthly series released from November 1999 to February 2000. $3-4each CRP
 (www.Pokémon.com)

Pokémon Video Mini-Comics
 Issues #1-7
 $15-16 CRP

Electric Pikachu Boogaloo #1 comic book by Viz Comics. $3-4 each CRP

Pokémon Game Boy Red cartridge by Nintendo. $30 CRP

The Pocket Monster Game Boy video game was Nintendo's first Japanese offering in 1995. Japanese children had their choice of Green, Blue or Red Pocket Monster game cartridges. These could be linked together for battle. Making the trip to America first was the Game Boy Red cartridge. This was followed by a Blue cartridge, which was a repackaged Japanese Green cartridge.

In Japan, the cartoon series, prominently featuring the yellow electric mouse Pikachu, was followed by the release of a Yellow cartridge for the Game Boy system. The Yellow cartridge paralleled events in the animated series. American stores received this version in time for the Christmas 1999 shopping season. (Brokaw, et al. 1999, 139)

Also available for the Color Game Boy system is Pokémon Pinball. This "Game Pak" has a built-in rumble feature new to the system. As the Poké Ball bounces around the screen, the game shakes in your hands. At present, this product retails for $30 and is too current to have a secondary market (collector's) value.

Offered on the home video system, Nintendo 64, is Pokémon Snap. This game involves luring some 63 Pokémon out into the open through bluff and guile with the assistance of apples, smoke bombs, dash engines, flutes and similar objects. Once exposed, high quality photographs must be taken of the Pokémon in action. The better the shot, the higher the score. (Brokaw, et al. 1999, 121)

Also available from Nintendo is the Pokémon Pikachu Virtual Pet. The ever popular, eternally cute Pikachu performs a number of different activities with your help. This game is currently priced at $20 in the retail outlets. It is too soon to provide a secondary market (collector's) value for this item.

Pokémon Pikachu virtual pet by Nintendo. $20 CRP

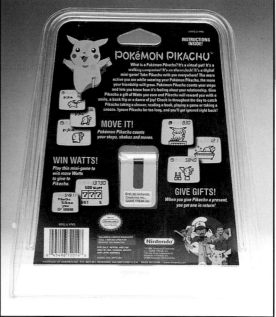

Poké Plush

A number of plush figures of popular Pokémon characters have been produced by Hasbro. These figures come in several sizes and more are likely to be on the way. Among the plush figures available at the time of this writing were:

Blastoise 8" Plush Doll	$15-16 CRP
Charmander 12" Plush Doll	$25-30 CRP
Charmander 5" Plush Doll	$10-11 CRP
Charizard 5" Plush Doll	$10-11 CRP
Eevee 5" Plush Doll	$10-11 CRP
Jigglypuff 5" Plush Doll	$10-11 CRP
Meowth 12" Plush Doll	$25-30 CRP
Meowth 5" Plush Doll	$10-11 CRP
Pikachu 14" Plush Toy	$45-50 CRP
Pikachu 9" Plush Toy	$11-12 CRP
Pikachu 5" Plush Doll	$10-11 CRP
Pikachu 3" Plush Key Ring	$4-5 CRP
Poliwhirl 5" Plush Doll	$10-11 CRP
Snorlax 5" Plush Doll	$10-11 CRP
Squirtle 12" Plush Toy	$25-30 CRP
Squirtle 5" Plush Doll	$10-11 CRP

#25 Pikachu Plush by Hasbro. Once upon a time, a flying squirrel—Rocket J. or Rocky by name—entertained TV viewers with misadventures and wonderfully bad puns. Today Rocky is replaced by a mouse with an electrifying personality—Pikachu by name. $11-12 CRP

Jigglypuff 5" Plush
Doll by Hasbro.
*Courtesy of
www.zapptoys.com*
$10-11 CRP

Five inch Pokémon Plush Dolls by Hasbro. Top: #25 Pikachu,
#06 Charizard, and #07 Squirtle. Bottom: #52 Meowth, #133
Eevee, #61 Poliwhirl, and #143 Snorlax. $10-11 CRP each.

Toys & Trinkets: Of Balls, Battle Figures, Blasters, Playsets ... AND MORE!

BANDAI

Bandai of Japan has released one inch high plastic Pokémon upon America's shores! Between 18 and 20 of the tiny plastic monsters come in either Pokémon Monster Trainer - Yellow or Pokémon Monster Trainer - Orange. These sets retail for $20 each today.

HASBRO

Hasbro is the major licensee for American Pokémon toys. Here are their products and values.

Battle Figures

Metapod (#11), Butterfree (#12)	$15-16 MIP*
	(*Mint in Package)
Kakuna (#14), Beedrill (#15)	$15-16 MIP
Pidgey (#16), Pidgeot (#18)	$15-16 MIP
Rattata (#19), Raticate (#20)	$15-16 MIP
Pikachu (#25), Raichu (#26)	$15-16 MIP
Sandshrew (#28), Sandslash (#28)	$15-16 MIP
Meowth (#52), Gengar (#99)	$15-16 MIP
Psyduck (#54), Golduck (#55)	$15-16 MIP
Mankey (#56), Primeape (#57)	$15-16 MIP
Geodude (#74), Golem (#76)	$15-16 MIP
Evee (#133), Flareon (#136)	$15-16 MIP

Battle Figures with Poké Ball and Battle Discs by Hasbro. Left: #54 Psyduck and #55 Golduck figures. Right: #56 Mankey and #57 Primeape figures. $15-16 each MIP

A closer look at Hasbro's Battle Figures: Pikachu (#25) and Raichu (#26). *Courtesy of www.zapptoys.com* $15-16 MIP

Another closer look at Hasbro's Battle Figures: Meowth (#52) and Gengar (#94). *Courtesy of www.zapptoys.com* $15-16 MIP

Electronic Figures

Charmander (#04)	$14-15 MIP
Squirtle (#7)	$14-15 MIP
Pikachu (#25)	$14-15 MIP
Meowth (#52)	$14-15 MIP

Micro Playsets

Forest Adventure	$8-9 CRP (**C**urrent **R**etail **P**rice)
City Adventure	$8-9 CRP
Beach Adventure	$8-9 CRP

Forest Adventure micro playset by Hasbro with #25 Pikachu and #43 Oddish figures. The three available playsets may be linked together to create a "larger" micro playspace. $8-9 CRP

Poké Ball Blasters

Charmander (#04), Charmeleon (#05), Charizard (#06)	$15-16 MIP
Pikachu (#25)	$15-16 MIP
Poliwag (#60), Poliwhirl (#61), Poliwrath (#62)	$15-16 MIP
Squirtle (#07), Wartortle (#08), Blastoise (#09)	$15-16 MIP

Poké Ball Blasters by Hasbro. The back of the package show the different Pokémon offered with the set. Left: Pikachu (#25) figures packaged with the red Game Boy-shaped blaster. Right: Poliwag (#60), Poliwhirl (#61), and Poliwrath (#62) figures packaged with the purple blaster. *Courtesy of www.zapptoys.com* $15-16 each MIP

Pokémon Master Trainer Game

This board game, a Hasbro and Milton Bradley collaboration, currently retails for $15.

Pokémon Master Trainer Game by Hasbro/Milton Bradley. *Courtesy of the Adam and Matthew Whiteford Collections.* $15 CRP

Power Bouncers

Blastoise (#09)	$3-4 MIP
Charizard (#06)	$3-4 MIP
Charmander (#04)	$3-4 MIP
Dragonite (#149)	$3-4 MIP
Flareon (#136)	$3-4 MIP
Jolteon (#135)	$3-4 MIP
Mewtwo (#150)	$3-4 MIP
Pikachu (#25)	$3-4 MIP
Poliwhirl (#61)	$3-4 MIP
Squirtle (#07)	$3-4 MIP

(Lee's 1999, 102)

Power Bouncer, #134 Vaporeon, by Hasbro. The rest of the figures captured in Power Bouncers are shown on the back of the package. $3-4 MIP

Pokémon Power Bouncers: Dragonite (#149) and Jolteon (#135). *Courtesy of www.zapptoys.com* $3-4 MIP

Pikachu Power Bouncer by Hasbro, up close and personal. This Bouncer would be worth $3-4 MIP. *Courtesy of the Madeline N. Snyder Collection.*

TIGER ELECTRONICS

Pokémon Lighted Keychains

Jigglypuff (#39)	$6-7 CRP
Chansey (#113)	$6-7 CRP
Pikachu (#25)	$6-7 CRP
Psyduck (#54)	$6-7 CRP
Squirtle (#07)	$6-7 CRP

Chansey Pokémon light up keychain by Tiger Electronics. *Courtesy of www.zapptoys.com* $6-7 CRP

Pokémon Yo-Yos

These yo-yos light up and play music as they move up and down the string.

Blastoise (#09)	$10-11 CRP
Charmeleon (#05)	$10-11 CRP
Pikachu (#25)	$10-11 CRP
Meowth (#52)	$10-11 CRP

Meowth Electronic Yo-Yo by Tiger Electronics. This toy has flashing lights and sound to accompany it on its trip up and down the string. The back of the package shows the other Pokémon electronic yo-yos Tiger produced. $10-11 CRP

Bibliography

Brokaw, Brian and J. Douglas Arnold with Mark Elies. *Pokémon Trading Card Game Player's Guide.* Lahaina, Maui, Hawaii: Sandwich Islands Publishing Co., Ltd., 1999.

Gutschera, Robert. *Pokémon Rules. Version 2. Trading Card Game.* Nintendo, Creatures, Gamefreak. Wizards of the Coast, 1998.

Lee's Action Figure News and Toy Review 82, August 1999.

Lippman, John. "Pokémon's Invisible Champion. Licensing Agent Bet on U.S. Kids and Scored Big." *The Wall Street Journal.* August 16, 1999.

Pulliam, Susan. "Pokémon Craze Produces Some Bears." *The Wall Street Journal.* August 26, 1999.

Snyder, Jeffrey B. *Collecting Star Wars Toys. 1977-Present.* Atglen, Pennsylvania: Schiffer Publishing, 1999a. 2nd Revised Edition.

_____. *A Trekker's Guide to Collectibles*. Atglen, Pennsylvania: Schiffer Publishing, 1999. 2nd Revised Edition.

There are also many excellent web sites where additional valuable Pokémon information may be found. One that this author found particularly useful was www.Pokémon.com.

Trainer's Notes

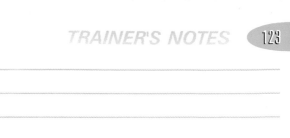